A Gift for Jesus

Coloring & Activity Book

I LOVE YOU, JESUS

Illustrated by Deb Johnson

30580PO100000051

After Jesus was born, wise men from the east came a long way to find Him.

Help the wise men reach Jesus.

The wise men worshiped Jesus.
Then they gave Him three special gifts:
gold, frankincense, and myrrh.

When we give gifts to the people we love
at Christmas, we think about the gifts
the wise men gave to Jesus.

When Jesus grew up, He gave an even greater gift than a Christmas present. Jesus died on the cross to save us from our sins. What did Jesus give us?

Write the first letter of each picture to find out.

Jesus is in heaven now. We can't give Him a Christmas present to show how much we love Him.

What gift can we give to Jesus?

Our gift for Jesus is not an object like a new car or phone. Our gift is what we give, how we live, and what we do. What did Jesus say?

Use the code to find out.

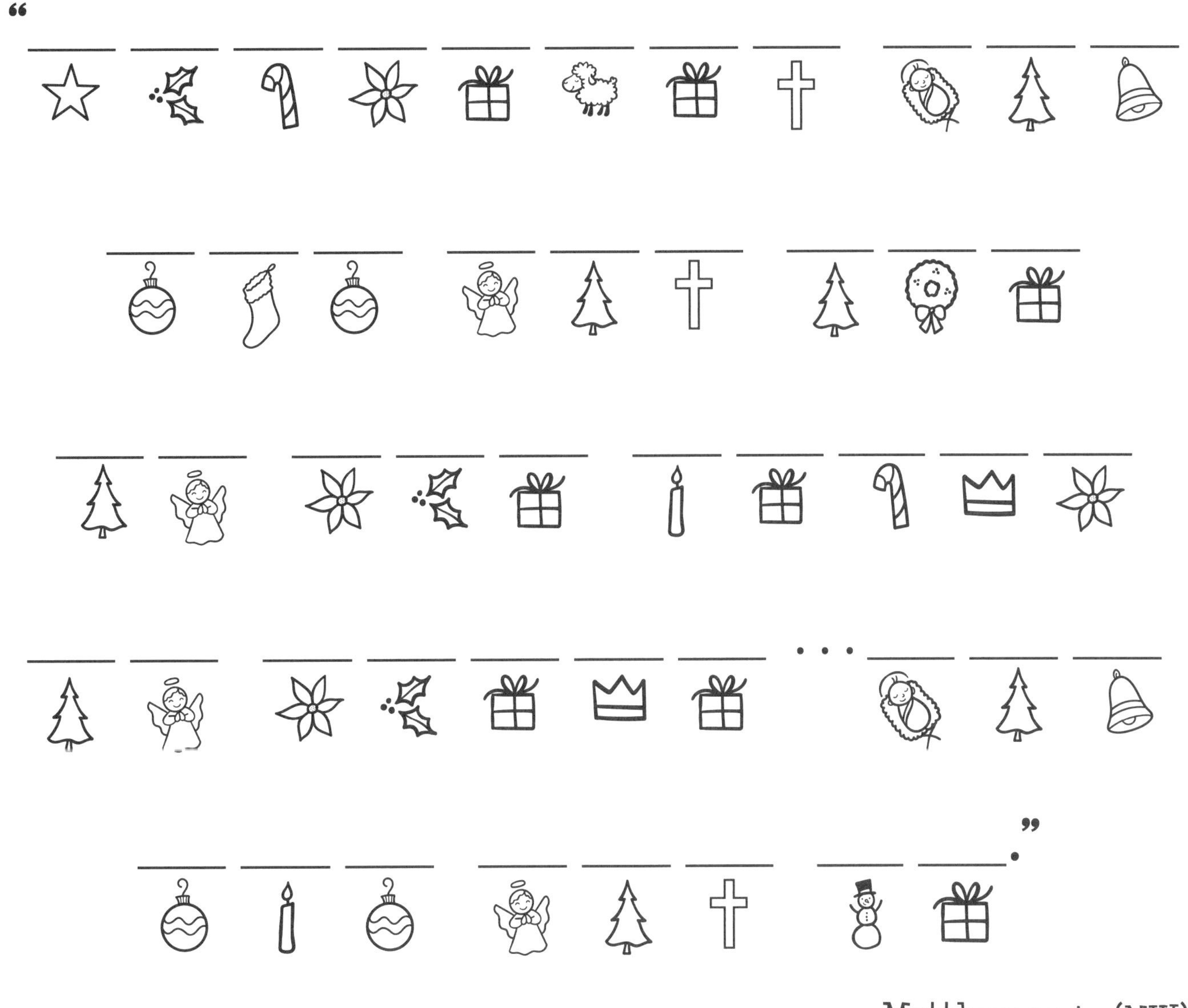

Matthew 25:40 (NIV)

A= E= R= O= W= D= F= L= M=

T= Y= V= U= I= N= S= H=

When you help a kid who is younger than you, you are giving a gift to Jesus.

Draw a line to match the words to the pictures.

When you help an older person, you are giving a gift to Jesus.

Find your way through this maze of good deeds.

When you take your dad a drink on a hot day, you are giving a gift to Jesus.

Find and circle the underlined words in the puzzle.
Words may be hidden forwards, backwards, up, down, or diagonally.

C E R T A I N L Y Y G K F S E V I G
U E J T B N D G G K X E I T U R Z T
A C A I S J L W K K D N B D K O F D
D N Z Z W D N O H I K C R M L Q O R
P K Y P U N Z E S M Q N N X N O L A
Q C P O O R T K Q E F N M T F D C W
K D Z S N I T N K B G X B L O T R E
E Q R I P E X E Z O Y C R L Z O T R
Z E M Y X R S V F G D I R C Q K T C
P D K J U K B E T P G E Q H R P U C
Q B E C E N N Y I B T T I O X D M G
S P G B T Z S A P G J N D A Q J
M M C X T X W R B E S H V C C O

"If <u>anyone</u> <u>gives</u> <u>even</u> a <u>cup</u> of <u>cold</u> <u>water</u> . . . that <u>person</u> will <u>certainly</u> not <u>lose</u> their <u>reward</u>."

Matthew 10:42 (NIV)

When you give a meal to a hungry person,
you are giving a gift to Jesus.

When you give clothes and toys to a family in need, you are giving a gift to Jesus.

Connect the dots.

When you visit a sick friend,
you are giving a gift to Jesus.

When you talk to a lonely neighbor, you are giving a gift to Jesus.

Which path will lead the kids to their neighbor?

When you save money and send it to a missionary far away, you are giving a gift to Jesus.

Do you know what gift Jesus thinks is best of all?
It's the gift of your heart!
Jesus wants to be your Savior and Friend.
He loves you so much!

The gift of God is eternal life through Christ Jesus our Lord.

ROMANS 6:23 (NIV)